LOOK . . . LOOK AGAIN!

CARTOONS BY
JOHN O'BRIEN

BOYDS MILLS PRESS
HONESDALE, PENNSYLVANIA

Text and illustrations copyright © 2012 by John O'Brien
All rights reserved
For information about permission to reproduce selections from this book, please contact permissions@highlights.com.

Boyds Mills Press, Inc.
815 Church Street
Honesdale, Pennsylvania 18431
boydsmillspress.com
Printed in China

ISBN: 978-1-59078-894-3

Library of Congress Control Number: 2012936283

First edition

10 9 8 7 6 5 4 3 2 1

Designed by Barbara Grzeslo
Production by Margaret Mosomillo
The titles are hand-lettered. The text is set in Times.
The illustrations are done in pen and ink and watercolor on bristol board.

CONTENTS

THE MOON

THOCK
THOCK
THOCK

THE ICE ROUNDUP

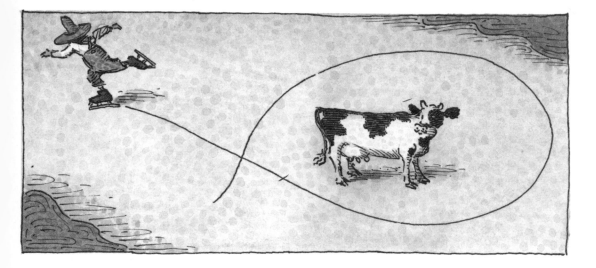

THE DAIRY COW

THE CHEF

THE CHICKEN DANCE

THE WAITING STAFF

THE PIZZA

THE ALPHABET SOUP

THE HOLLER TREE

THE QUARRELING WOODSMEN

THE WOODSMEN'S HATS

THE PALM TREE

THE KNIGHT

THE KNIGHT AND THE DAMSEL

KNIGHT WEAR

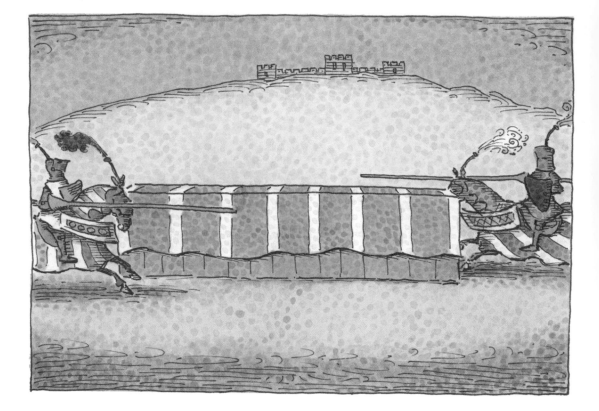

THE JOUSTERS

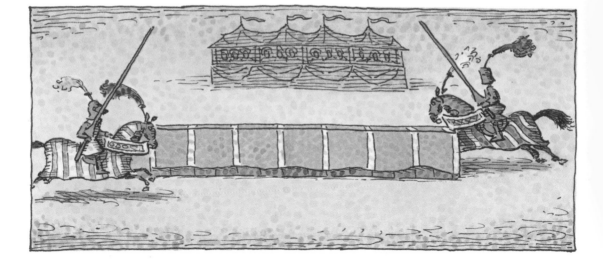

THE ROUND TABLE

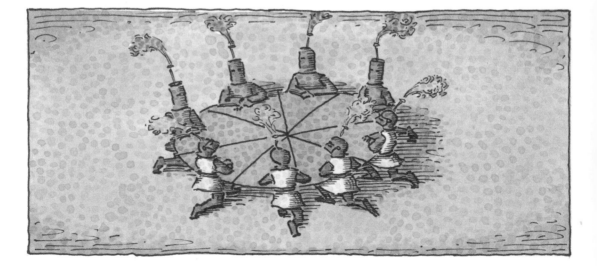

THE DOORMAN

THE AUTOMATIC DOORMAN

THE SNORER

THE NEWSSTAND

THE AWNING

THE LOWN

THE THREE-RING CIRCUS

THE FOOT RACE

THE BALLOON HAT

THE FLAT TIRE

THE TV SET